T0366170

ONE

ONE

Marwa AK

PARTRIDGE

To order additional copies of this book, contact
Toll Free 800 101 2657 (Singapore)
Toll Free 1 800 81 7340 (Malaysia)
orders.singapore@partridgepublishing.com

www.partridgepublishing.com/singapore

Contents

Introduction

Poetry has a way of speaking directly to the soul. This book resembles pain yet it isn't painful. Sometimes all we need is to write our feelings down to feel a little lighter on the inside. Maybe a whole lot lighter. "One" is a geographical home for hope, dreams, reality, pain, tears, joy and sorrow. All these feelings and emotions have One thing in common, which is, they don't last. Nothing in this life is forever. Any emotion ever felt can last for a minute or days. It is within our power to let go or hold in. The reason I decided to name my humble collection of poetry "One" is because everything in my opinion at the end equates to one. The power of One!

On another note one cannot go through the struggles of life all by themselves. Team work is the key for a successful business. The famous line of "One hand cannot clap alone". We all need that other person or group of people that helps us overcome all the down feelings we're going through. Hand in hand we are one. Always remember the Hand of God is with the congregation.

I would like to end my introduction by dedicating every word written here to my family, friends and love of my life. At my lowest and my highest moments, I've always found in you a shelter from the rain.

Always One,

Marwa AK

Hope

When the sky brings color to your day
With every sunrise and every sunset
When the wind blows directly to your face
With every teardrop running down your face
Blame it on the weather
When you are not the same person you used to know
With every feeling ever felt, remained untold
Weighs on your shoulders like a thousand stone
When the whole world becomes a lie
and your eyes search for truth
You will find that hope lies within
Therefore,
"Hold On Pain Ends"

Unexpected

Just when I have given up hope
You came back from nowhere
With a two words text
All this time I spent to stand up
Went to waste
It took a moment to fall back
On my knees
Deep in my being an earthquake
Took place
Wounds in my heart reopened
I thought they healed
I could feel it beat in my ears
I could feel it bleed in peace
Cold war they call it
Hurting me in silence
Feelings awoke from yawning sleep
Memories grew hands
And they're pulling me
Out of this mess
I have nothing for you to see
I built a wall
That you can't break
Not with your empty words
Nor with your pity on me
Not even my yearning
can break it
The broken me
You will not perceive

No More

Excuse me
if I talk too much
All I said and done
wasn't enough

I told you I won't let go
until you hear me out
But you left no room
for my thoughts to come out
How dare you say there is
nothing more to be said
How could you judge?

I'm the one
The one that remained
Remained unsaid
I'm no words
in your game play
I play no games

The time has come
to stop waiting on time
to undo what is done
What once was will never come
I will let you walk over my lands
No more

I'm the king of this castle
And I've closed behind you the door
Leave, don't forget
to count your steps
on your way back home
Days I've counted your absence
are forever gone

Finding New Land

I want you to know
I was doing okay
Not like you care
I was just fine
Until.

Until I don't know
I saw your face
You looked at me
And drove by
My darling you
Need to stop causing me pain
I need to let it go
And let it be

You are no longer my man
on the moon

See I look outside the window
Stare at the crystal sky
Feel the wind fly through
My fingers as I reach
Out my hand to hold you

I keep busy
I ignore my mind
Yet every light in the city
Food chewed with my teeth
The movement of noise
The sound of silence
Everything carries me to you

It's like everything that exists
Knows you

I want you to know
You shook my ground
But I am going to be the man
Wake my buried legs
Carry my roots
And find a new land

What the Tree Said to Me

I'm sitting on a five step stairs
My behind is starting to get sore
Staring at the big sad tree
at our front door

I wish I was this tree
Let my hair dance with the wind
like it leaves do
I wish I was this tree
Sad enough yet it stands tall
I wish I was this tree
Be a shade to those who care
I wish I was this tree
A home for birds

The tree kneeled down
Looked at me with sorry eyes
She said
We're no different
We both have seen it all
From stormy weathers to blazing sun
And the rain washed us one too many times before
Look at me, I lose my leaves every fall
In winter it gets too cold
Don't wish to be me
I've got no place to go
You got a choice between being a tree
Or just letting go

Why Love?

Thoughts in my head
Words filling up my chest
Mouth sealed with broken feelings
Empty eyes
Loud silence filling the air
Very heavy to breathe
Silence is silent
Even on windy days

The weather is clear now
I can see crystal clear
I can see you crystal clear
So blindly
I don't need to close my eyes
Every time I miss you
You are there in my arms
Making me love you
Beyond my mended heart

How did I forgive you?
After all the damage done
You didn't have to say you're sorry
You only showed up
And I took you in my chest
Felt your breath on my skin
Your kiss on my cheeks
Your fingers loving my hair

Yet here we are
In the same old page
Afraid to be a written book
Afraid to say who we are
Two people in love
Why Love?
Do you make us do foolish things
Brave enough to overcome pain
Cowards enough to accept the pain

Why Love?

Don't Cry

Young girl don't cry
He may have did you wrong
But don't let that affect you
He may have taken you for granted
But don't forget yourself now you
The present is your gift
Don't live it with regrets and sorrow
Your smile is brighter than the sun
It can't be hidden even if he
forced a cloud on to you
Lift your head against the sky
Learn the birds' song by heart
Sing your silence till it echoes

Big girl don't cry
Your biggest sin you've fallen in love
with the wrong person or two
Learn to forgive yourself
God will forgive you
Isn't that a reason to move on
Show him who's strong, yes it's you
No man is worth the rain, the pain,
the holes you dig in your chest too
Let the beast in you awakens
Time to crush them mountains in your way
Walk over the graves of buried hopes
Today you celebrate no longer being a shadow

I

I lied to myself
This is what I do
I became a liar now
Look what you've done
to me
I am here, but there
I am not me
I am here, but there
I count days
Keep dates
In my memory
Little by little you will grow
out of me
Another lie.
I hoped
Little by little I will defrost
My frozen feet
And walk from the empty shore
Of broken waves
I piled oceans in me
And lost me
I, I, I…
I am sick of saying I

Wish I could say 'we'
What about us?
What we were meant to be
Wish I could say 'you'
To find you
Your hand in mine
Walking each other to the sun
We shine
How beautiful would it be?
But you left me by the shore
To sail a different sea
With a broken back
And tired arms grown long
trying to reach you
I pray you find
Something bigger than your ego
I pray I find
Something other than your silhouette
to cling too
Something more real
Someone ready to contain me
From me, (I)

Missing You

I am back on my back
Laying down like that
My head hurts
and I have coughed
once or twice
I don't know if it's the
body ache
or the days that passed
Without a single word
from you
I need some time alone
but you refuse to leave
my thoughts
I don't feel well
I'm turning in still ground
I let my hair loose
and my head I'm about
to lose
I worry
another day will pass
without a word
from you
So I go back
to the wishes I never had
I wished for a walk
by the beach with you
I wished to lay down on grass
with you
counting the stars

I wished for a photographed
picture with you
All these clichés
A bunch of romance
I wished all that
Now there's no proof
we were together
But it's no excuse why
are we ignoring each other
Just come back
I will let go of all that
Cause missing you
hurts more than
a fairytale
I'm waiting to live
Come back
Cause missing you
hurts more than the
words you did not say

Missing you,
means a lot more than
the empty relationship
I assumed we had

Untitled

I can tell a story in three lines:

He said she's worth it, she believed it
He asked for time, she gave it
She asked for a minute, he denied it

The End.

I Am Nobody

Today passed
Tomorrow came
And I haven't heard from you
in days
Tell me now,
how is this fair?
Hating all my friends
for being there
While you're not
What's their fault?
It is not your fault
I am the one to blame
for giving you more than
my capability of giving

Yesterday
I walked away
Without a single word said
You failed to hear my silence
Muted by your own
confidence that I am
here to stay
Look at the miles
between us I am standing right there
beside you
You're too blind to feel

my existence
Truth is I lied
I haven't taken a step
away from you
But the distance is
a walk of thousand days

A year in time
I wrote dozens of poems
about leaving you
And today, here I am
Still I am
But my words ended
Emotions even tears can't describe
Everything needs to be said
is heard in songs
Felt in the wind
that crushes my chest
You seem to breathe
a different air
My oxygen comes
from grass
Yours from glass
Cause you're the man that breaks
And I am nobody

Almost a Love Letter

My Dearest,

Read the words
read the lines
or read between the lines
Whichever way you want
Whichever way, you can
skip the lines
but don't skip over my heart
it beats for you
As cheesy as it sounds
I have lost my mind
over you
lost my sight, my knees too
All I got left is a red pen
it bleeds letters of pain
I never knew
So I write
in disguise
Hoping one day it will reach
you
Look up to the sky,
tell me do you see my face
a shining star
I've seen your face under every sky
over every sky

You are that man on the moon
Reach to the river,
tell me do you feel my tears
with the waterfall
Sometimes I feel you fall (for me)
with a little tenderness
Most times I feel you far (from me)
with a lot distantness
I don't want to feel
I want to know
I deserve to know
what is it you hide
behind the mountain (between us)
what is it you fear
a distance of forests (between us)
Now tell me, my dear
is this love?
or am I asking too much?
All I ask is to hear
the words that belong to my ears
I am going deaf hearing
loud silence...

Sincerely,
Empty words

Distance

Days like this
I lay on bed
Having conversations with you
in my head
Where have you been?
How have you been?
How foolish of me?
I saw you in my future
You're not even present in my present
I am starting to feel that I built you
with my imagination
But you are real
So real
Don't you remember the first time
you put your arm around me
It was a matter of minutes and you had me
Don't you remember our last time
you had both arms around me
I memorized every beat of your heart
my favorite melody

Days like this
I remember when I wanted to leave

You made me stay
Where are you now?
Don't I deserve a goodbye?
You said I am worth it
What am I worth to you?
What is worse that I am answering
the questions I asked you
This time
Oh baby this time
I won't blush and freeze when you
say you want me
I am done falling
You won't even have me tripping
I bought new feet
I am done drowning
You won't have me shuddering
like a fish out of water
I learned to swim off your sea

...I missed you, but
the distance you created between us
is bigger than how I feel

Silly Poem (Colors of the Rainbow)

Roses are red
Violets aren't blue
The sun shines in yellow
And sets in orange
Yet this is not a reason to fall for you
The traffic light went green
That's no reason too
to sneak your fingers between mine
While I was shifting the gear
from neutral to drive
I don't want to go there
A feeling a silly poem like this
can't describe
Maybe I'll just add one more color
Indigo,
So I can tell you I painted a rainbow
for you

Three Words

I can tell a story
Beginning, climax, ending
Between the lines a hidden path
Round and round
A circle made of glass
Only way out is by breaking
Make it a home
The truth is a lie
Imagination is real
Nothing makes sense
Right is wrong
Left is right
Love is the same
Feelings become untouchable
in time
Destinations changed
Limited on words
Pages remain white
Leave the book open
Everything starts, ends...
with you

All She Wrote, All He Read

Take off the mask nobody is watching
Frown that smile the eyes are talking
The person in her, crumbled standing
The beast in him, a beautiful king

She wanders in search of a mountain
She buries a feeling bigger than words attain
She shivers inside a dancing fountain
She smiles like there is no pain

He holds a mountain
He holds the words
He holds a fountain, the pain
All in the palm of his hand

She believes it not
A listener to silence he is not
The mess she is with an ocean hugged
Shattered peace in her deep got lost

As she wears back her mask
The eyes blink and shush
All he holds slips of his hand in rush
She rise to let the person in her crush

Pretenders

Let's take a walk back
back to memories from not too far
yet they are in black and white
let's walk back
before silence filled the air
before the wind got heavier
as it touched their face

Gravity is lost in space
hearts beating out of pace
it was wrong to smile
but it seemed like the only right thing to do
what felt like far far away
is just one step away

Let's stop pretending
this is about me and you
stop coming back like everything is okay
There is a lump in my chest
your hand is squeezing my heart
like you want me to stay
a feeling only if you are able to see
you would know

Now that I walked away
and we said our goodbyes
good
what is not good that I haven't found closure
what is not good that what we had
was nothing, to walk away from
You have built me higher than I could grow
and just left me there
with no foundations
so I fell off

I only have one more thing to say
you are a song
I never got a chance to learn by heart
funny thing is
I am the writer of that song

Walls

There is no law of physics
No trick of magic
No illusion
No water
Not even reality
Can go through the walls you've built

No it is not a dream!

Imagination led me to an extreme
I've led it beyond me
I no longer want to hide behind words
Seems like my thoughts are betraying me

Will it make sense if I say it as it is?

You don't hear my silence
I don't understand yours
You don't question my absence
I resent yours
You don't feel my pain
I doubt yours

Questions I wanted to ask you

A volcano in my chest?
Or a freezer to my heart?
Which weather do you want to put up too?
Is it time for a joke?

Nothing will break the ice you're beyond cold
Nothing will break the walls you're beyond bricks and stones
Nothing will heal the unspoken words to be told

March

Every red light
A scent of a perfume
Turquoise a reason to smile again
Choke on words
A feeling bigger than me

Was it your voice?
Or the messages till dawn?
Wake me up before the sun
Hear me say hello
A feeling bigger than you

I used to sing
A song of youth
Now I long
A kiss on her cheek
Oh that day how much I hated my hair

Believe me you
A story been told
'What is real now was once a dream'
It's the opposite with you
It was real
Now it's just a dream
A feeling bigger than us

Maybe tomorrow I'll write
With love
It's not just a month
It is forever

Once Upon a Time

Once upon a time
A boy found a girl
She was lost in her head
He thought he could get her to his head
Let's have a conversation he said
Her reply was I rather play a pretend game
I don't mind as long as we're communicating let's have it your way
What do you want to be he said?

Girl: let's pretend I'm the ocean and you're the sky
Boy: nice, at least we have the same color in common
Girl: but your blue has white clouds and they bring out rain
Boy: so? You reflect me day and night, whether I'm blue or
    black
    And you have white too, have you forgotten your waves?
Girl: my waves are not a reflection of you, that's how I feel
    sometimes I am calm sometimes I rage.
Boy: what angers you my darling? I promise I'll kill it right
    away
Girl: my ocean is filled with fishes; don't try to find my way.
    Sharks smell blood, don't be "killing it" you'll end up
    hurting yourself
Boy: I want you
Girl: have a good day

Days pass and the boy find the girl again,
Where have you been he said?
I'm here where you left me don't come near me, I'm an ocean
with rough waves she did not say.

Boy: I miss you

Girl: I had your reflection on me all day. But some of your clouds turned gray. I remained blue just like oceans always stay.

Boy: are we still in the pretend game?

Girl: we're not pretending I'm the ocean you're the sky, your clouds seemed like they will rain today.

Boy: whatever you say

Boy: I really miss you; let me swim if you're an ocean as you say

Girl: I'm a deep ocean, if you can't swim you would drown and I have no hands to pull you away

Boy: laugh out loud, I would love to drown in you it would feel great...

Months pass
Boy finds himself lost in her head

The story never ends
This is the way it goes

Once Upon a Time Part II
(The Story Ends)

There was *once a story told between a boy and a girl*
They found each other in a dark dawn in spring days
They shared a story of an ocean and a sky, a pretend game
And thought it would never end
Here they are, separated
By the distance of words they left unsaid

Their last conversation made the night scream where do I go with all
the memories? I don't like dark days...

Girl: What is wrong with you? I called many times. Tell me
    what happened?
Boy: I have nothing to say.
Girl: Talk to me
    What changed?
    It's been a month, without a word from you.
Boy: isn't it over, you said. What do you want me to say?
Girl: No it is not I can't let go of you *she did not say*
    I told you I am upset cause you've been away
    Then you disappeared for twenty days
Boy: I was busy with my friend, I apologized you didn't
    accept it
    And you were dry about it
Girl: saying sorry isn't enough; I waited day and night for you
    to show me
    I put up with your coldness for a year did you hear me say
    a word?
    I sneaked out on dark nights to see you
    All I asked is a minute of your time
    She again did not say

Boy: Do you want to go back to being an ocean? I am the sky?
    Okay let's pretend, how do you feel now?
    Girl: No I don't want to pretend. I…
Boy: Okay this is for the best trust me, let's go our separate
    ways
    There's nothing wrong with you. It is I
    You deserve better than me
    I am not ready for anything
    All the break-up lines he said
Girl: but I don't want anything
Boy: I know. I wish you all the best
    I swear you deserve better

*The girls' heavy breathing filled the silence on the other side of the
phone
Moments till she found her voice and managed to say*

Okay, Thank you

*The pain found place in what she left unsaid, her head screamed I
have a voice, hear what I have to say. Don't listen to her silence. I
want to be an ocean, I miss my sky. I want to be an ocean, I miss the
color blue with all its shades. I am no longer a sea I'm just a drop lost
in the waters of time. I want you back as a solid; I don't want you a
cloud in my dreams. I miss you and I miss us as painful as it was.
Please let's start over, I promise I'll give you more space, more than
the distance between the ocean and the sky.*

Boy: You're welcome.

The End

What I Know About You

I know you're the summer, you got me sunburned by the look
of your eyes
I know you're the winter. It rains so much
It's not about the weather baby
It is about what I know
I know you're a painter, how you draw a smile on my face
I know you're a poet, words you never say I feel in my heart
I know you're a joker, I laugh at the excuses you make
I know you're a love song, I dance with the shadow of lyrics
I know you're an empty book, white pages I flip trying to find
three words that belong to me
I know you're a dream, I happen to be awake
I know you're an earthquake, yes I shake!
What I know about you, you disappear but you're here

I know so much it makes me wonder...
What do you know about me?

You Chose Nothing to Say

Sometimes, sitting alone is dangerous
My brain takes me by surprise
It wanders off to unfamiliar places
You are everywhere I go
I think I need a mind shift
Why do you do this?
A question I ask myself regardless

Sometimes, sitting alone is marvelous
My heart takes me by surprise
I realize that you couldn't care less
Still you are everywhere I go
I think it is time I care less
What is this?
I am starting to repeat myself

If I to start all over again
Would it be cliché if I said?
I put up against fire for you
You wouldn't stand for me in the rain

Would it be cliché if I said?
I'd walk a thousand mile just to see your face
You wouldn't log in to skype to see my face

It doesn't matter what I say
It matters what you say

You chose nothing to say

Upon My Imagination

Over time dreams became facts
Spent my life as a dreamer
Reality never made an impact
Does that make me an imaginer?
Words I never found
Many times I thought of never coming back
You make me stay in a certain state of mind

They say collecting pieces is the cure of a broken heart
Chasing is not any fun until you catch
Or shall I imagine that you hold my heart?
Cry me a river
You have ripped me apart
Roses by the dozen won't bring me back

You take your time
I patiently wait, lost in my own thoughts
Properties I never owned
Why is it that I only write when I am confused?
Emotions I never felt
You bring that to life
With lies you never told

It is a small world
You fit in it perfectly
I live in wonderland
A place you gave me with all your heart
Not enough space to hold my heart

Sand

Just like the sand of shores
Waiting for a wave to pull me to the unknown
Just like the sand of shores
Sometimes I'm soft, sometimes I'm rough
Just like the sand of shores
I'm full of shells, I hide in those

My smiles made of tears I moaned
My eyes speak the language of silence
My heart beats inside out all day long

If I were to feel I'd touch a cloud
Get wet in the rain
Soak in the sun

If I were to play a wish game
I'd wish me much as I was ever wished good
I'd wish I never met a reason that stripped me down naked in
space of 'could'
I'd wish I never smiled a tear over you

You are the reason I should
Just when I start to wander off in my head
You pull me back to the ground of delusion

Just like the sand of shores
I'm too many
Count me up if you dare too

Shaded Reality

I've looked everywhere in search of home
Years I've longed
Pretending I am the strongest
Truth is I'm just numb
Till the day magic woke my senses up
It was a matter of time, I lost sight
It didn't matter as long as I felt
Is it me? Or the sun got out of sight
It didn't matter I let the sun shine in my heart
What heart?
I have pieces
Seems like luck not good at playing puzzles
Does that make me out of luck?
They say people learn from their mistakes
What does that make me that I have learned none?
I am a lonely ocean I've lost my shore
I am a lonely desert my sand is gone
I am a lonely star, can't see me even when it's dark
I am a lonely book I ran out of words
Truth is I am just someone who thought that had found love.

Shore

If I can hug the shore
Hear the sound of my heart through a seashell
Dream deeper than the ocean
Leave home
Never look back
I would
Because I need to feel the unknown
I need to free myself
A prisoner of thoughts
A wanderer in lonely lands

We're Through

Conversation between her and him

I know I said it once, twice, and three times before
I don't want you no more
I have deleted your number a thousand times from my phone
If love is blind
How come you're everything I see?
If time is lost
Why do I always find my way back to your arms?
It's been five years now
And silence is all I can feel
How come you don't want me no more
Where I provide everything you need

Baby it's all in your head
You shouldn't be asking how I feel
I don't have to say a word
You already know what you mean to me
You are my hero, my superwoman
Sometimes silence speaks louder than words
And I honestly have nothing else to say
I am not ready for this
With you I can't even compete
Don't ask questions you won't like the answers too
I don't see you in my future, no

Sometimes I need to hear you say it
I am being fooled with what I see
Cause my heart don't beat faster when I hear your voice
And I don't get nervous when we touch
Nothing feels the same
Is this really over? I'm scared to admit
Wipe the tears of your face
I don't want to cry
It hurts to stay
So you're going to have to watch me leave
If you ever need me, you know I'll always be here

I am sorry, I am sorry, so sorry
I said it out loud, I am not going to see you again
You are my shelter
You are the hug that I miss
The kiss that I crave
You are my favorite smell, my favorite voice
You are the only one that saw my tears
You are truth, my realist
I am the man I am today because of you
All these feelings, it's called being human
But baby, maybe it's better if we both go our separate ways

Love Me

Time is running
Forever is short
So this is it?
We made it to the end
Deep down I knew we never were
All ends need beginnings
Though we never started
So how this could be it?
It's been months
And I'm starting to give up on you
Even though it hurts
Sometimes I wish I could
Get rid of you
With all my fears
Fears of losing you
Truth is, you lost me
When you had me all at once
Once upon a time in love
I was the only one
But baby I am alone is not enough
I needed to hear you say it
Say you love me
Make me weak to my knees
And I'll forget all the unsaid words
Like they were never heard
Say you love me
Replace the tears of my smile with teeth
Like I never cried

Friend

I'm no good with people
I don't do parties
Or play house
I don't tell the funniest jokes
Nor I laugh out loud
I'm boring as it gets
And play Sudoku for fun
Spend my most hours alone
Never ask for help
I don't need someone to understand me
I struggle with that myself
All I ever wanted is someone
who comes in
When the whole world has gone out
That is a friend

Future

All I ever wanted was to make my father proud
I have walked a million miles
Felt the heat of the deserts burn through my lungs
I chased the light before sunrise
If this is a dream come true
Then it's stupid because nothing makes sense
I don't want to wake up in the morning
My stomach lost its butterflies
I failed my friends
And oh yes failed in love
Just so I don't fail myself
But what for?
I failed in life
I miss my brothers
I miss when I was young
When everything tasted good
When I knew how to smile
I look at old pictures and cry
Makes me feel so old now
Whoever said the future is bright
Told a lie
Because the future is now
And nothing feels right
My ground shakes below me
Struggling to find feet
To walk that extra mile

Happy Birthday

Twenty six a number
Wish it ends here
Times add but it lessen in years
Maybe I should stop counting
Maybe I should start again
Less is more
Time reveals
People never count
Family stays real
The more I give
The less I receive
It's not about quantity
It's what one feels
Prayers for the Man above
Thank you for who I am
For all the blessings beyond me
Why celebrate one day a year
Where every day is a happy birth of me

White Dress

If you ask me what is my greatest sin
My answer would be
Falling in love with you
If you ask me what will I do over and over again
My answer would be
Falling in love with you
Baby we've been hurt, I've been confused
But every time I try to forget you
I find myself in your dreams
What is it that you do?
that makes me come back to you
I can't say we're made for each other
Meant to be together
Clichés in songs that we listen too
Yet I pray that we do
In reality I'm crazy for you
And you're crazy for me
Your eyes say it even when you
hide behind your ego
Now let me ask you
if love isn't crazy then what is?
If our time ends here
I know in another place
In another time
Our crazy will end with me in my white dress
With you in your black suit

Until another time
Let's be stupid in love
With no reason and clue.

Cinderella

Roses are red
Violets are blue
Forever she shines
Though forever is through
Every beauty needs a beast
The beast needs beauty too
Dozens of time wasted
Time to get true
Roses by the dozen died
Once or two
They say third time is a charm
His charm has gone few
The clock has ticked
It is midnight at noon
If time is everything
Cinderella would never lost her shoe
I am no princess
I got both feet in my shoes

Truth

No matter how dark the night is
The sun will eventually shine
Starry winter days warms with a lovers touch
Spring flowers blossom with a butterfly's touch
It takes a minute for a heart to pump of chest
With butterflies in stomach
Next March will eventually come
Then the eyes can speak the truth
That love is a lie

Calling

I am here
Where have you been?
I've been waiting for months for you to call
Only yesterday I decided to be the bigger man
I called you with nothing to say
I heard your voice and started crying
Remembering how it all began
Four years ago at the movies
You've put your arm around me
Ever since you owned me whole
Why am I the one saying sorry?
When you were the one that broke me all
I'm ready to pick up the pieces
I am here
Calling, to ask
Let's go to the movies and do it all over again
You can put your arm around me
Break me again
Cause baby every time I tried to leave
I fall back into your arms
Stay here
How could you walk away?
Leaving me with nothing
But pictures on my phone
Don't you know I miss you?
I don't have to tell
This is all I am
Making it easy for you to love me once more

Beautiful

Here's to a dream
Of being everything I can
The moon, the stars don't compare
To your face
A smile with dimples
That cares
So when the day is over
And the night is cold
Do me a favor
Look in the mirror and say
I am beautiful
Cause you are

Here's to a wish
Of strength so divine
The sun, the rainbow don't compare
To your soul
On fire you are
Happiness is you
In and out
Pass it on to others
Like candy bars
Now look at the mirror and
Tell me how beautiful
You are

Hero

He moves mountains with a touch of his hand
He lends his chest for shelter on cold nights
He breaks all silence without saying a word
He is a sweet kiss, the one that feels like home
He is the way home
He is a Hero
The only one she's ever known

Time Keeper

Turn off the lights
Let me see where I am
Five years passed
We're back to square one
Did time actually move?
Or stayed still?
Honey, time flew by us
We are still
Five years passed
We haven't flipped a page
Still stuck on empty words
And a lump in the chest
Turn off the lights
Let me wake up from this dream

Stranger

A stranger to my eyes
A stranger to my soul
You're everything I've ever known
Stranger than the sun to the moon
Your voice no longer feels like home
Strangers we've become
Since you decided
to play cold

Lost

I don't know how to feel anymore
Making up excuses for you in my head
Some days you're here
Most days I am searching for you
in every sunset
I don't know how to feel anymore
I've lost every sense of logic in me
with you leaving
It's not only my rules you've broken
My ego you underestimated
It's all my fault
I ripped myself into pieces to keep you whole
I don't know what to feel anymore

Love Is Just a Word

Love is a verb
With you, it was just a word
Never said
You said silence speaks louder than words
In our case
Silence was just silent
Nothing heard
Everything painful felt
If every poem ends at a lump in chest
You are an empty poetry book
I have written you
With every choke on words
Tears excelled
Maybe
This is the end.

Dreams

I may have asked you to leave a hundred times
You may have walked away a hundred and one
Walking after you in a maze
And I can't find my way out
I too am amazed by how puzzled you've become
Months I have longed for a word or a surprise visit
You only know your way to me in my dreams
There's where you visit me much
In my awakening I have missed your touch
My forgiveness you dream
I have buried my softness such
as it can't visit you in your dreams
Even if I wanted too
Reality deeper than dreams
I have swam oceans of promises
My beautiful patience has dried out
My heart is an empty water well
That you can't fill with a painful look of your desert eyes

One

Here we are in this dark room
My heart about to fall out of my chest
with every beat
On my back turn me around as you please
Let my hair fall down as we reach
each other in space
For the fire in us will finally speak
Your fingertips brushing every part of my skin
On my knees and I no longer feel my feet
Let me sing through your ears
You are mine and this is real
Your body over mine I could barely breathe
As we touch we become one
This is eternity
The night is ours I don't want you to ever leave
Lift me up I'm in your dreams
Hold me tight make me scream
Let me drown in your arms and lose gravity
You are my hero
You can easily save me

Empty Words

Tears dry on their own
Mine dried but I'm sobbing inside
What else can I say?
What more can I write?
The aching within me
Needs more than a thousand book
Memories of years
Chasing a word
Feelings involved
I feel like a naked body cut into pieces
With a cold sword
Listening to the voices inside a thunderstorm
The ship has sailed into the ocean
Reaching for land
This story has been told
Nothing left to hear
Except these empty words

Sighs

All I ever wanted was to make the child me proud
Old now and not so proud
Yet not old enough
For this sorrow and stress
I'm the ocean, deep
But not enough for these tears
A change is going to come
Though it may take years

Blue

How long has it been?
I tried to forget
Pretend like I lost count
How long I try
You will always be the love of my life
The one that broke me to pieces
I see your face in every person I meet
Hear your voice in every story spoken
Even in the darkness of my closed eyes
Your picture brightens up my vision
I'm blind
You're everything I see, the people no more
I cry tears of painful joy with the thought of you
They are called memories
Oh how I wish I can build new with you
But the weather is against us
And a million miles distanced by ego
Through the rain I'm offered a hand of umbrella
I may neglected one or two
Waiting for you
To shelter me from this rain
And the cold wind as it hits my spine
Making me weak for you
What if the winter ends?
Then the summer shines my days
Warms my nights
And I no longer need you?
Let this sink in for a minute
As I swim the oceans under your skies
Both in the color blue

Beauty and the Beast

She wears a smile too beautiful
It's unmatched
He wears a face too sharp
It breaks hearts
Her heart is broken
For the words of love
He's never spoken
She drowns his oceans
He knows she owns him
Though this fact she doubts
His ego too big it carries mountains
For the words of silence
He screamed out loud
As the sound of emptiness echoes in their hearts
Their brains rage the way out
Prisoners of pride
A beauty queen she is
Inside out
One look of her eyes melts a man's soul
For the sun sets in her eyes
A beast he is
With a gentle touch
He holds the world at the palm of his hand
One step of his foot he crushes every woman's dream
Like the sun and the moon they never meet the same time
Though the moon dies with every dawn to give the sun its
breath
Worlds apart
Together they will forever belong
Because,
Every beauty needs her beast

Woman

I am a woman
I move mountains
I fight the with every breath
I build legacies in a day
Turn the world around as I swing my hair
I am a woman
I come, see, and conquer
it all
Untouchable, I'm too high
You can't reach me
even if you learned to fly
Knock me out
You can't break my walls
Unbreakable
Though I am made of glass
I should be handled with care
I own a smile so bright
The sun resembles my shine
I am woman
With the darkest side
The stars need my darkness to shine
I melt ice with a look of mine
For the sun sets in my hazel brown eyes

Meet Me in Your Dreams

Every story has its wounds
Ours was never told
Everything we were
Remained in the dark
We could be classified a lie
For that my heart is forever scarred
Listen to me
When I tell you
You are the love of my life
You may not hear it twice
I care not for your pride
Push me away
Further than the sun
Your arrogance won't hurt me
I am detached
Beyond that
I am confident enough
Ten years from now
You would sit by the shore
Smiling to the wind
Reminiscing my love to the ocean
Mourning the hate you had for sand
Wishing you could go back in time
To get your feet dirty with mine

As we walk through the oceanfront
You will look around in search of my scent
Paint your walls black to the color of my hair
Get mad at your feathered pillow
For it's not soft as my skin
This is when you will realize
I am everything you ever dreamt of
Now there are tears dripping down your face
As you close your eyes to sleep
So you can meet in your dreams

Printed in the United States
By Bookmasters